In the forests of California and Oregon stand the tallest trees in the world. A redwood tree may grow to be more than three hundred feet tall, with a trunk that is ten feet thick. It takes about five hundred years for one of these beautiful trees to reach its full height, but some of them live on for more than a thousand years. In a redwood forest you may see a tree which began to grow centuries before Columbus came to America.

David Adler describes how these giants of the forest live and grow to their amazing size, and what is being done to protect them. Kazue Mizumura's handsome illustrations portray the redwoods in all their majesty.

by *David A. Adler*   illustrated by *Kazue Mizumura*

Redwoods

Are the Tallest Trees in the World

Thomas Y. Crowell Company · *New York*

LET'S-READ-AND-FIND-OUT SCIENCE BOOKS

Editors: *DR. ROMA GANS*, Professor Emeritus of Childhood Education, Teachers College, Columbia University
DR. FRANKLYN M. BRANLEY, Astronomer Emeritus and former Chairman of The American Museum—Hayden Planetarium

LIVING THINGS: PLANTS

Corn Is Maize: The Gift of the Indians
Down Come the Leaves
How a Seed Grows
Mushrooms and Molds
Plants in Winter
Redwoods Are the Tallest Trees
    in the World
Roots Are Food Finders
Seeds by Wind and Water
The Sunlit Sea
A Tree Is a Plant
Water Plants
Where Does Your Garden Grow?

LIVING THINGS: ANIMALS, BIRDS, FISH, INSECTS, ETC.

Animals in Winter
Bats in the Dark
Bees and Beelines
Big Tracks, Little Tracks
Birds at Night
Birds Eat and Eat and Eat
Bird Talk
The Blue Whale
Camels: Ships of the Desert
Cockroaches: Here, There, and
    Everywhere

Corals
Ducks Don't Get Wet
The Eels' Strange Journey
The Emperor Penguins
Fireflies in the Night
Giraffes at Home
Green Grass and White Milk
Green Turtle Mysteries
Hummingbirds in the Garden
Hungry Sharks
It's Nesting Time
Ladybug, Ladybug, Fly Away Home
Little Dinosaurs and Early Birds
The Long-Lost Coelacanth and Other
    Living Fossils
The March of the Lemmings
My Daddy Longlegs
My Visit to the Dinosaurs
Opossum
Sandpipers
Shells Are Skeletons
Shrimps
Spider Silk
Spring Peepers
Starfish
Twist, Wiggle, and Squirm: A Book
    About Earthworms
Watch Honeybees with Me
What I Like About Toads
Why Frogs Are Wet

Wild and Woolly Mammoths

THE HUMAN BODY

A Baby Starts to Grow
Before You Were a Baby
A Drop of Blood
Fat and Skinny
Find Out by Touching
Follow Your Nose
Hear Your Heart
How Many Teeth?
How You Talk
In the Night
Look at Your Eyes*
My Five Senses
My Hands
The Skeleton Inside You
Sleep Is for Everyone
Straight Hair, Curly Hair*
Use Your Brain
What Happens to a Hamburger
Your Skin and Mine*

And other books on AIR, WATER, AND WEATHER; THE EARTH AND ITS COMPOSITION; ASTRONOMY AND SPACE; and MATTER AND ENERGY

*Available in Spanish

Library of Congress Cataloging in Publication Data   Adler, David A.   Redwoods are the tallest trees in the world. (Let's-read-and-find-out science books)   SUMMARY: Describes the characteristics of the redwood tree. 1. Redwood—Juv. lit. [1. Redwood] I. Mizumura, Kazue. II. Title.   QK494.5.T3A34   585'.2   77-4713   ISBN 0-690-01368-X (lib. bdg.)

1 2 3 4 5 6 7 8 9 10

Redwoods
Are the Tallest Trees
in the World

LET'S
READ
AND
FIND
OUT

The tree near my house is so tall that I can't even reach the lowest branch. The top of the tree is higher than my house. It is the tallest tree on our street. But this summer I saw trees which were much taller. We went to California and I saw the redwoods. They are the tallest trees in the world.

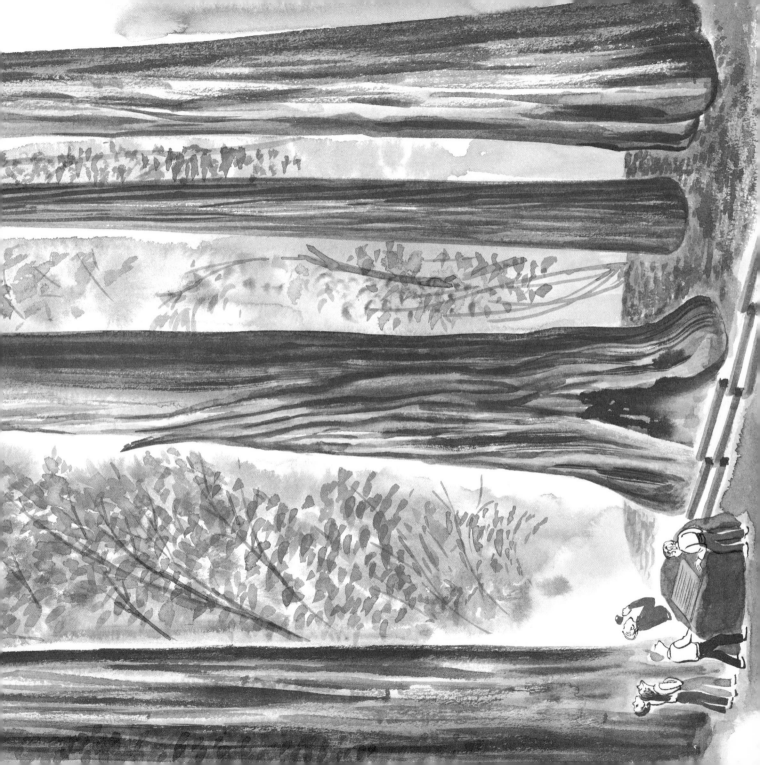

We saw them in a national park in California. The ranger told us that redwoods need a lot of sunlight and water. They grow best where it does not get too hot or too cold, and where there is a lot of moisture in the air. The climate on the northern coast of California and in southern Oregon is just right for the redwoods.

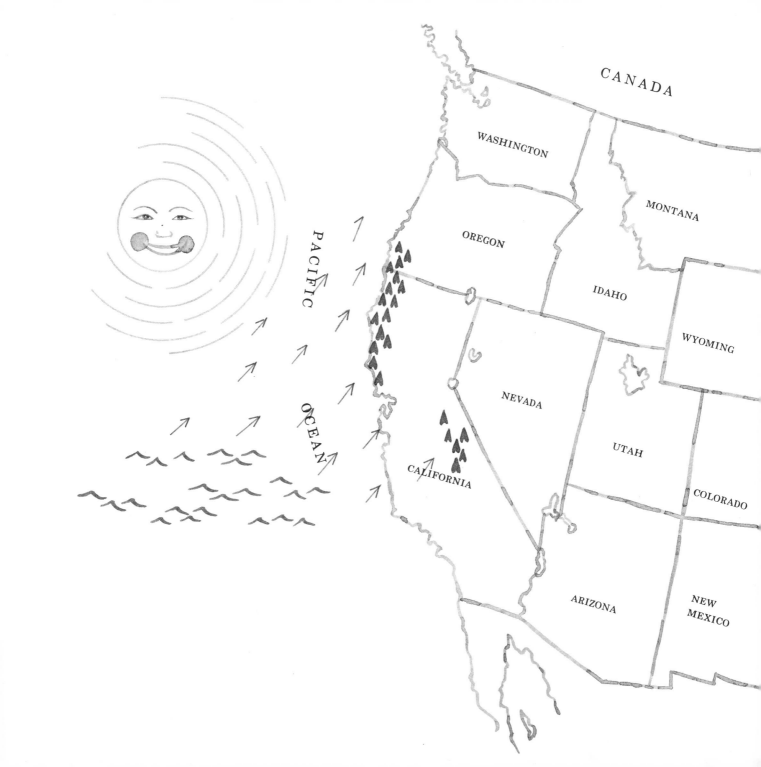

The ranger also told us that redwoods grow about ninety meters high. That's over three hundred feet. The tree near my house is only about fifteen meters, or fifty feet, high.

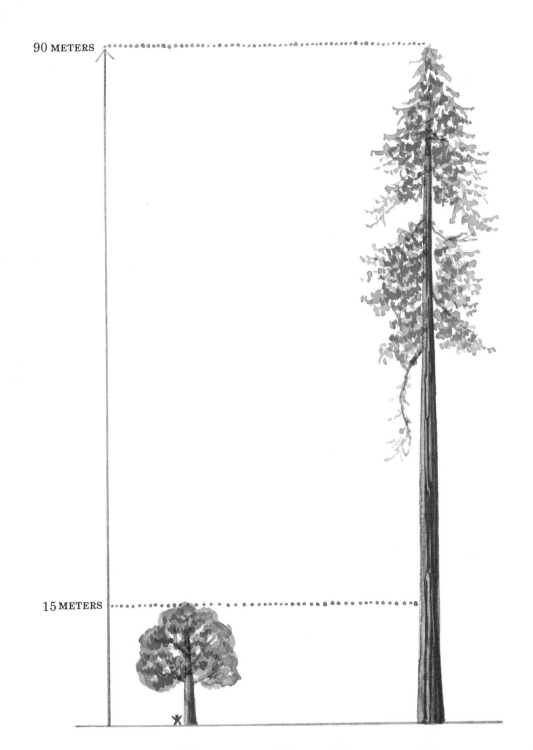

90 METERS

15 METERS

7

Redwoods are members of the sequoia family of trees. They are named for Sequoyah, who was a leader of the Cherokee Indians. There are two kinds of sequoia trees. *Sequoia sempervirens* is the scientific name for the redwoods. *Sempervirens* comes from the Latin word for "ever green." The other kind of sequoia tree is *Sequoiadendron giganteum. Dendron* means "tree" and *giganteum* means "big." These are the biggest trees in the world. They have larger trunks than the redwoods. But even the "big trees" never grow as tall as the redwoods.

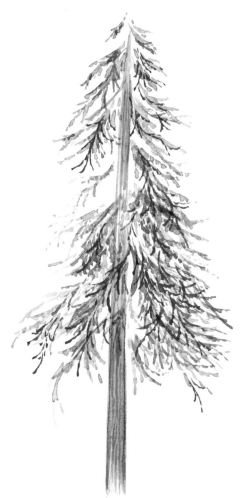

Sequoia sempervirens

Sequoiadendron giganteum

9

Redwoods are evergreens. They have small needles which stay green all year. At the end of the redwood branches there are small round cones. Each cone is about the size of a large grape.

The cone holds about fifty seeds. Each seed can grow into a tall redwood tree, but few of them do. Most young redwoods grow from the roots of other living redwood trees or from the roots of redwoods that were cut down. The old roots take water and minerals from the ground and help the young tree grow quickly.

Many young trees may grow from the roots of just one old tree. We saw redwood trees growing close together in groups. They probably all grew from the roots of the same tree.

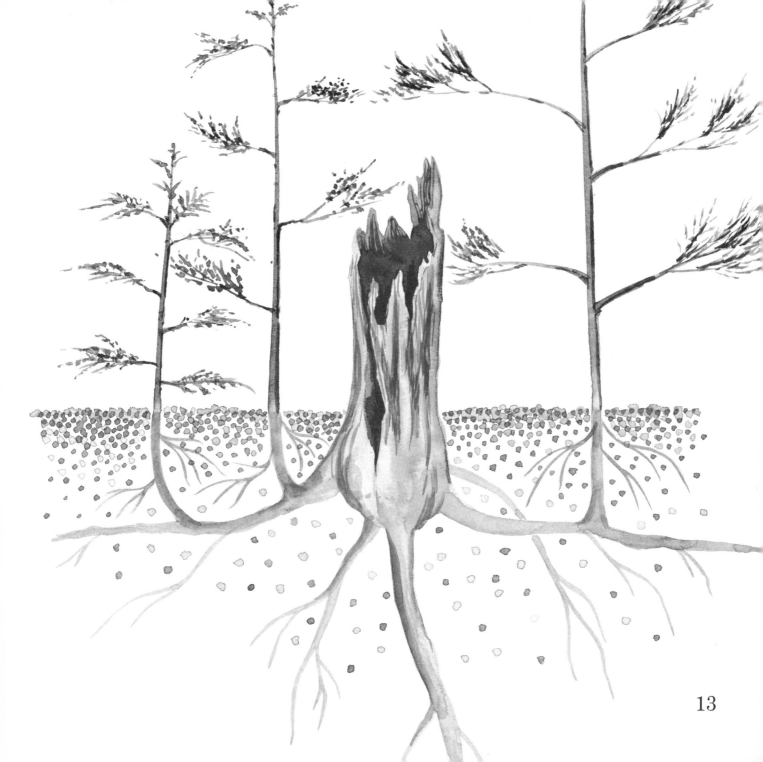

13

New branches grow at the tops of young trees. These new branches and the branches of other trees keep sunlight from reaching the redwood's lower branches. The lower branches die. Some very old redwood trees have no branches at all for the first thirty meters, or about one hundred feet.

15

It takes about five hundred years for a redwood to grow to its full height. But many redwoods live longer than that. Some redwoods live more than a thousand years. After that the tree begins to die slowly from the top. Sometimes its branches are killed by wind or lightning. Sometimes the tree is weakened by age or fire. Then it is no longer able to send water all the way up to the top branches.

When a tree has been cut down you can see the rings in the stump. Tree rings tell us how old a tree is. The width of each ring shows how much the tree grew during that year. Sometimes the weather is so bad that a tree grows very little. There is no ring for a whole year. At other times, when the weather is very good, two rings may form in a single year. But years like that are unusual. Almost always the number of rings tells us the age of a tree. And the width of the ring tells us whether the tree grew fast or slow.

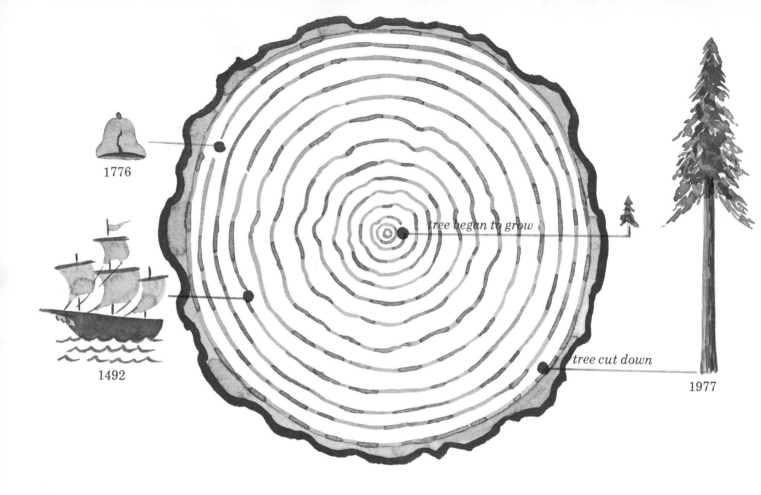

1776

1492

tree began to grow

tree cut down

1977

The ranger showed us the stump of a redwood tree. It was about three meters or ten feet across. This tree started to grow over one thousand years ago. It was more than five hundred years old when Columbus came to America.

20

I couldn't count all those rings. Maybe at home I will find the stump of a younger tree and count its rings. Branches have rings, too. You can count them and see how many years the branch grew.

The bark of a redwood tree is sometimes almost thirty centimeters thick. That's nearly a foot thick. This thick bark helps a redwood live for such a long time. The roots of a tree collect water and minerals from the ground. The water then travels up the tree trunk to feed the branches and the leaves. It travels through layers just under the bark. The bark protects the layers.

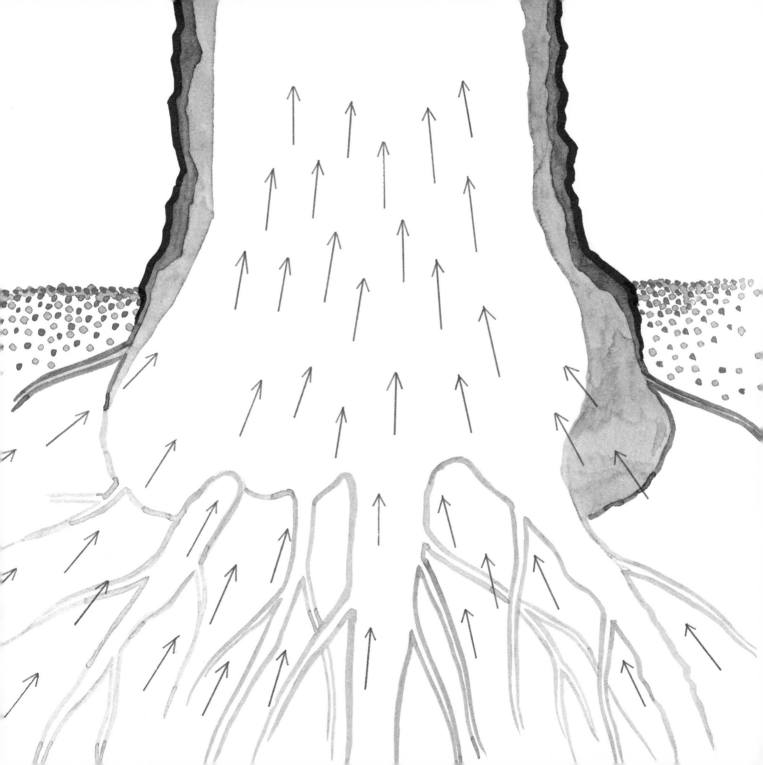

Because the redwood's bark is so thick it also
helps protect the growing part of the tree from
fire.

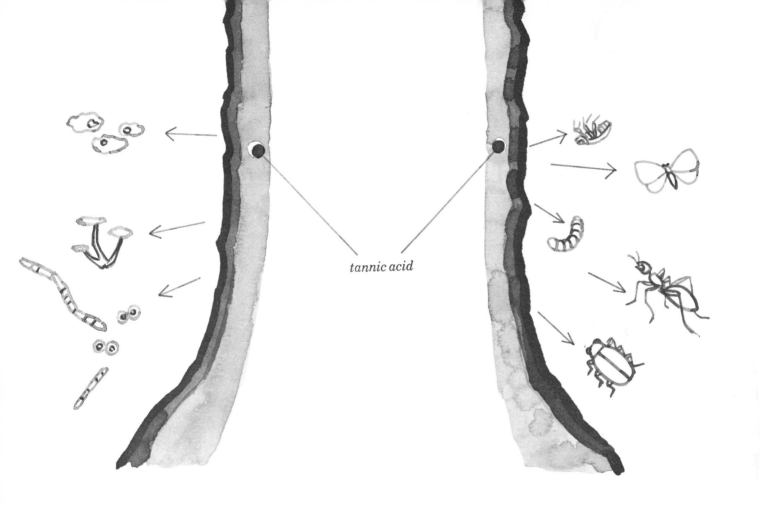

tannic acid

The redwood bark contains tannic acid. This protects the tree from insects and disease.

On the bark of some redwood trees I saw big bumps. The bumps are called "burls." Burls do not harm the tree. They are really redwood buds that did not grow into branches. The burl is hard and beautiful. Some of it is even used to make jewelry.

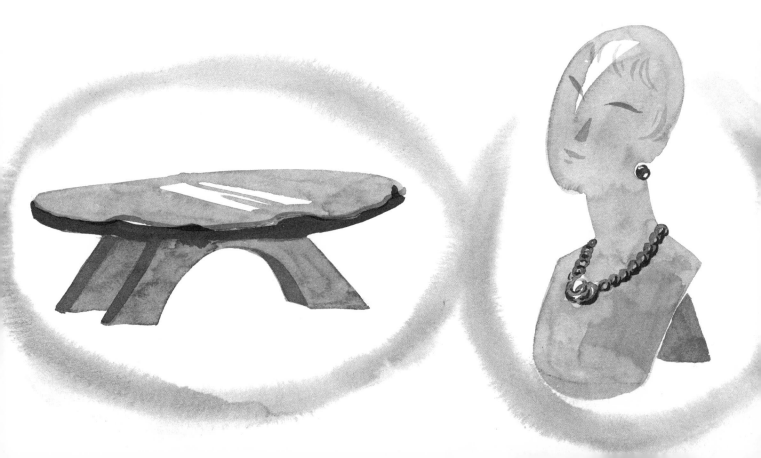

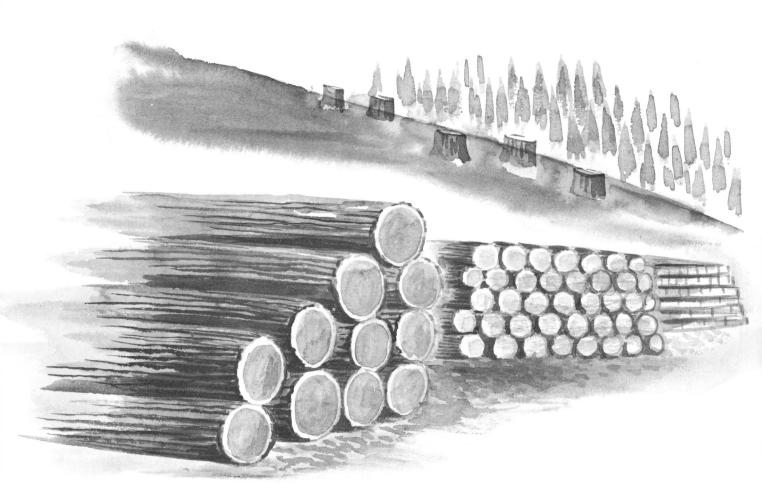

The wood of a redwood tree is very strong. Things made of it last a long time. Redwood lumber is used to build houses, to make indoor and outdoor furniture, railroad ties, and much more.

Because redwood trees are so tall and
straight there is a lot of valuable wood in each
tree. Sometimes there is enough wood in one
tree to build four houses.

People are afraid that too many tall redwood trees will be cut down for wood.

To protect these trees the Save-The-Redwoods
League buys redwood forests and makes them
into parks.

Redwoods are the tallest living things in the whole world. Here I am standing in a redwood forest. You can see the trees but you can hardly see me. Next to a redwood almost anything looks small. If you ever see one you will know what I mean.

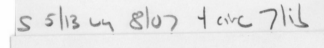